Contrary to expectations, *After Lunch with Frank O'Hara* is more like a Monty Python send-up than a nostalgic paean. Craig Cotter has come through his emersion in and admiration of the famous poet to create an original and gleeful collection of poems that disarm, challen~ ~nd amuse. Duende, a gesture in art, such as a mistake ~~ ~ ~ allowed to show when passion breaks ~~ ~) façade, is usually associated with mor ~~~ or lyric poetry, but Cotter uses it consis ~~~ etimes shockingly, to indicate his assu~ ~~art, and to break with it in order to claim his ~~~ent Craig Cotter voice. In so doing Cotter is defiantly, passionately, and of course a little sadly, leaving Frank O'Hara. His "lunch" with O'Hara was a meal of using one's friends and daily life as a grid for learning aesthetics. The desert was a very rich confection made of gay love. Having taken this sustenance from O'Hara, Craig Cotter is one well-nourished poet. Read this book like coffee and conversation that follows a great meal.

—Diane Wakoski, author of *Bay of Angels* and *The Diamond Dog*

i'm just an old straight prof emeritus & sometimes Craig Cotter's poetry gives me the creeps & sometimes its vulgarity qualms me & sometimes its translucence is a stained glass window i don't want to look through / a revolving lucite door i don't want to spin through, but man it's riveting as it forges itself it's written in gists & piths as he speaks with straight Creeley & queen O'Hara & others as the subversive who can't never get enough he wants "submissive twink" & tells us he "jacked off 6 times yesterday" to composites of guys & tells us in a fantasy idyll that Marlon Brando told him "u could not be an artist / if all you cared for was convention and laws", & how much cum & how many blowjobs & dicks are too many as Cotter challenges us not to run the fuck away from his obsessions & to know his big-hearted Whitmanian embracements & adhesions his camerado tendernesses too so look & hear all sorts of ravelings & unravelings of Beauty here in this prodigious poet of crafted outpourings & i want i need always to be erect & wear his poems to new graduations because my doctoral hoods & gowns thanks to him gaily shred

—William Heyen, author of *Shoah Train: Poems* (National Book Award Finalist) & *Straight's Suite for Craig Cotter & Frank O'Hara*

After Lunch
with Frank O'Hara

Craig Cotter

INTRODUCTION BY FELICE PICANO

Chelsea Station Editions
New York

Published by Chelsea Station Editions
362 West 36th Street, Suite 2R
New York, NY 10018
www.chelseastationeditions.com / info@chelseastationeditions.com

Print ISBN: 978-1-937627-18-8
Ebook ISBN: 978-1-937627-54-6
Library of Congress Control Number: 2014939873

Cover and book design by Peachboy Distillery & Designs

These poems were previously published in the following publications: *Alimentum*; *Ambit* (London); *The Antigonish Review* (Nova Scotia, Canada); *Aufgabe* (Issues 7 and 9); *BOMBlog*; *Caliban Online* (Issues 4 and 6); *Cokefishing in Alpha Beat Soup*; *Court Green* (Issues 6, 7, 8 and 9); *Dalhousie Review* (Halifax, Canada); *Eleven Eleven*; *Euphony*; *Global Tapestry Review* (UK, Issues 31, 32 and 43); *Hamilton Stone Review*; *Hawaii Review* (Issues 71 and 73); *Hazmat Review* (Vol. N, Issue 1 & Vol. 11, Issue 2); *Inkwell*; *Jones Av.* (Toronto, Vol. XIII, Issue 4 and Vol. XII, Issue 21); *Krax* (UK); *The Los Angeles Review*; *Lungfull!*; *Margie*; *Marymark Press* (Give-Out Sheet Series); *Mudfish* (Issues 16 and 18); *Nexus*; *Nimrod*; *Ottawa Arts Review* (Canada); *poems-for-all*; *Poetry New Zealand* (Issues 36, 38 and 42); *Rune* (Issues 29 and 32); *Transcendent Visions*; *2RIVER*; *Van Gogh's Ear* (Paris); and *Urban District Writer* (UK).

for Robert Creeley

Contents

Introduction

Knowing Frank

by Felice Picano

A mid-season episode of the highly praised Home Box Office dramatic TV series *Mad Men* has its identity-challenged protagonist, Don Draper, reading a small book of poetry with a dark blue cover outlined in red, the 1964 City Lights first edition of Frank O'Hara's *Lunch Poems.* We first see it while he is at the desk in his office at the Manhattan advertising firm where he works, then later outside while he's having lunch. Further into the episode it is prominent on his office coffee table and even on the commuter train as he's headed home. It's a clever way of placing the character and the episode at a specific point in time, and an even cleverer way of setting up Draper as a successful creative advertising director and as someone who is trying to be in-the-know.

The choice of *Lunch Poems* sets Draper up as an open-minded character, not quite an intellectual, but at least a man with some contact with and context of the avant-garde of his era. O'Hara's book of poetry was the opposite of the accepted poets of his day, such as the confessional and anguished poems produced by likes of Sylvia Plath and Anne Sexton. Instead, O'Hara's poems were fun, amusing, citified, arty, casual, urbanely referencing singers, painters, and even brand names that every one did or should have known. At all times, his book was intimate and confiding, letting the reader into the poet's emotional and daily life, not recollected in tranquility but with wry amusement between sandwiches and martinis. It was the definition of that *Playboy*-era's highest compliment: cool! So it was no surprise that when Don Draper was divorced the following TV season, he moved to the West Village.

In the mid-1960s after finishing college and a few months in Europe, I moved west myself to the Village, from Manhattan's Alphabet City, where I'd previously lived. At twenty-one, I was on my own in Greenwich Village, already a legendary Bohemia, in a third floor studio apartment at 51 Jane Street.

My second day residing in the Village was a perfect autumn one in New York: sunny, with high clouds, breezy and so clear I swore I could make out the Hudson River, several blocks west. After lunch, I took a long walk around my new neighborhood, and two blocks from where I'd moved I met a tall, blond curly-haired, handsomely outgoing young man who told me his name was J.J. Mitchell.

As we were talking, he angled me into a doorway on an otherwise empty street and began assiduously necking and fondling me, which I found both surprising and welcoming. Satisfied with what he'd discovered, my new acquaintance walked us over to the large glass and travertine lobby of a building at Jane Street and Eighth Avenue known as The Rembrandt. We necked more in the elevator, outside an apartment door, and then we were suddenly inside an apartment where a cocktail party was in progress. Men were jammed into a large room and an attached kitchen. Everyone held a cocktail and everyone was talking at once as loud as they could and laughing.

J.J. vanished and reappeared with cocktails for both of us. He then edged me over to another doorway, urging me to drink up. I thought this was odd, but okay: *I'm willing to do this, if he is.*

I was maneuvered through the door and into a darkened room and spun around. Another man was sitting on the bed and, as J.J. continued kissing me, the man unzipped my fly, took out my genitals and began to .... Well, you can guess what happened next. This was even more of a surprise, but I was nothing if not game, even if I was a bit perplexed. I was even more puzzled when J.J. vanished from the room, while my new friend held onto me tightly. I was young and horny and he was demonstrating an admirable and accomplished skill, so let's just say that we completed what we'd begun with the usual result.

Afterward, my newer friend handed me my cocktail glass, stood up and said, "I need another. Thank you." He herded me toward the door and led me back into the party, adding, "Stay as long as you like. There are all kinds of interesting characters here."

I had to have looked as stunned as I was by this odd turn of events, but before I could decide what to do next I wanted to find what had happened to J.J. He seemed to have left—someone came over to me who I knew, a French airline steward named Ulysses, another tall, handsome blond with curly if thinning hair. He immediately kissed me on both cheeks and began speaking in Frenglish, the speech that he and his other pals usually affected in America. Ulysses said that our mutual friend, Noel de Bailhac, had stepped out with someone to get more ice. Noel and I had met at the Bethesda Fountain in Central Park the previous year and we'd casually slept together whenever he was on layover from Air France, where he also worked as a steward. Noel was a pretty man with a great body and lots of fun in and out of bed. In seconds, Noel and Ulysses' boyfriend were back with bags of ice, and I spent the remainder of the party in their ambit until we left to go around the corner to Greenwich Street to a little *boite* they knew, for dinner.

At one point, the man who had blown me also came into the café, along with J.J. and a few other middle-aged men. They were seated way in the back where they continued to laugh and chat and drink cocktails as everyone had done at the flat. Noel told me that he was our host for the cocktail party. He was revealed to be a bit below medium height, not yet forty years old, preppily dressed, with receding brown hair, a patrician face, sleepy eyes, and a great, almost Greek-statue profile. Noel said he was Frank O'Hara, a poet. Ulysses knew J.J., who was our age, from before; J.J. had stumbled across my French pals earlier that day in Sheridan Square and invited them to the party. Noel thought the other men with Frank and J.J. were painters.

Two days later, I was walking along Jane Street headed toward the Seventh Avenue subway when I passed Frank walking toward his building. He stopped me and said, "We're having a big party at Indiana's loft downtown Saturday." He pulled out a piece of paper and a pen and leaned against my shoulder and began writing down the address, saying. "I already mentioned you to Robert and he wants to meet you." Huh? What? Done, he handed it to me and I read the Bowery address. By then, Frank was already halfway down the block, yelling "Bring some of those other cute guys you know."

Noel and Ulysses were both flying that weekend, so I grabbed David Jackson, who I always thought was all-American handsome, and despite our misgivings about the Bowery space—"Won't there be winos and bums all over?" he asked fearful—we went. The space we entered was ten times the size of O'Hara's flat and it was jammed with people. We didn't see Frank anywhere in the crowd. David and I were about to leave after having had a few drinks and figuring out that we knew no one there when Frank showed up with a striking looking man his own age, but bigger, more solidly built, and really quite dashing in his black cowboy vest, open work shirt, and tight jeans. That was Robert.

David and I met seven other guys that early evening who asked for our phone numbers and over the next year we were invited to various parties, a gallery opening, and even to Bridgehampton for a weekend. In later years, people asked why I wasn't still hanging around with those folks. I explained it thusly—"At Southampton we would arrive for dinner at eight and have cocktails. At eleven thirty we were still having cocktails when I heard that someone had begun cooking dinner. At eleven forty two, they were still having cocktails but I was dead asleep."

At the time I wasn't aware of it, but I had also met other writers at these parties. In years to come James Schuyler, John Ashbery, Richard Howard, and others told me that they'd first seen or met me during my Year of the Painters.

Then came the awful news of O'Hara's death by taxi-cab on the beach at Fire Island. Me and my social worker pals used to take those taxis every Saturday from our Ocean Beach rental to the Grove to go dancing. Who knew they were so dangerous?

Of course by then I'd read the *Lunch Poems*, and O'Hara's *Meditations in an Emergency*. I was sorry I'd not gotten to know O'Hara better. But often I wondered if I ever could have—really. Because while only a decade apart, Frank's Gay New York was so fundamentally different from mine: they drank, we drugged; they had cocktail parties, we went out dancing; they had complicated affairs and adulteries, we had orgies; they had scandals, we had be-ins. In the later '70's and early '80's, through Edmund White's older friends, I was able to get to know a little better and thus to appreciate more Manhattan's gay generation before mine: I still can quote Schuyler and Merrill poems. But even so it was a foreign land: a land where *Lunch Poems* was the passport, the guide, and the dessert all at once.

So, you can imagine my surprise when Craig Cotter's *After Lunch* arrived by mail. I'm not sure who connected us up, but when we met after that, I already understood that I was encountering the biggest Frank O'Hara fan who ever existed. Hell, it turned out that Craig had even read the lousy poets that Frank had drunk cocktails with; that's how big a fan he was.

This new book of poems was for me an absorption and distillation of what Frank had been, wanted to be, and had written about—but decades later, set in Los Angeles's own quite different urbanity, and by a basketball playing, Beatles-addict from Michigan.

Dude! Seriously!

Oh, and Craig Cotter is also a good poet.

Enjoy.

After Lunch with Frank O'Hara

Awake

for Robert Creeley

Bernie took me to San Francisco

to meet Alan Segal
and his lab Cassidy
he taught to give blow jobs

The 4 of us walked through the Mission
Got the 3-pound clear plastic bag
of broken cookies at the bakery on

(I can't remember the street)
He stayed in a New College building
59 Lapidge Street. I showed up there 3
                                    years later

Alan was gone
but a perfect 18 twink
blonde, 5-7, 125

welcomed me

cocaine laced joint and bed.
But back to that trip
in your Camero back to LA

when I threw the pound bag of M&Ms
out the window on PCH
they bounced high, wild &
            colorful

off the engineering wonder
off the roofs & windshields of cars
            behind us
and everyone smiled

                My grandmother's raised
                            buckwheat pancakes
and maple syrup
still at 46 the best breakfast
        I ever had

that morning in San Francisco with you
in Chinatown
down to thirty dollars

White porcelain plate of scrambled eggs
and shrimp steaming with oyster
sauce for 2 dollars!

Four eggs fluffy, perfect, moist
20 large fresh shrimp
and my first thick, sweet
        oyster sauce from China.

The San Francisco air sunny,
            humid, cool,
you knew you were straight
I didn't know I was gay

I was 19
you were 20
watching men hold hands out the window

I had the street of that bakery
        memorized for years
the submission guidelines said unless
        you're Whitman or Ginsberg
        (both dead) no long lines.

We forget what we don't use

Dear Carrie

I invited him to my room:

Blander   [1969]
domed carapace
walking up Michigan woodland hill
        from breeding population swamp

Room of icons, relics, amulets.

Today
        all hepatica in Michigan alive
blend with dead leaves.

KJ walks stairs to my room

pieces of Pra Pathom Chedi, Doi Suthep,
the Berghoff, 2 pieces of his hair in a Thai jar:

How link 1969 to the Naka at Doi Suthep?
How purple Michigan wildflowers
to the foundation of Hitler's house at Obersalzberg?

I've got to find a tube of lanolin for Frank O'Hara.

Carrie how do you not make a mistake with that first new student?

Tolstoy gave one-and-a-half pages to the murder
of the 18-year-old boy tied to a pole by the French in Moscow.

An Intermediate Period might last three centuries.

I still want Alex up
he's 43
boyfriend when I was 16 and he was 14 he was always 3 inches taller.
Even if 40 more years
it's over already
toddler learning language
(ya ya ya ya) pretending it's a secret

Advice for Carrie Preston

I'm afraid I'll outlive Mano.
I don't want to bury him or see his dead body.
I don't want him to not be in my apartment.

Google hepatica, check it out,
find one in nature in Michigan, get back to me.

What else has been bothering me today?

*

You know not too much really.

I had a foot boy worship my feet, his name is Donald and he's a dancer too.
He likes jazz more than classical ballet
but he's studying ballet to improve his jazz.
Do you think that's sound advice? One of his teachers gave it to him.

Diane doesn't get
why I'm not going to defend or talk about my poems.
She gets why Allen Ginsberg refused to defend or talk about his poems,
in fact she defended his decision to not defend his poems.
While just sending me another email telling me why I am weak for
just letting the fucking poem stand.

*

A very very very very famous poet
wrote me I'm the only poet he knows who sends his first drafts to friends.
There are so many ways to interpret that.

Can we give advice that isn't directed at ourselves
or at our desire to create art or to search for whatever we are searching for?
Some days it's a flower, some days a foot.

The young boy Plato or Socrates studying in marble
at the Musée d'Orsay—there's a fine foot for you.
The whole piece is lovely too and no one knows the artist

the sculpture just appeared in the train station one day
and no one asked any questions.

I need to take some drugs to knock myself out.
Goo night sweet lady
and try to sort through this and give your life some fucking direction!

For Alex

My memories are lies because I lie every day and that has affected my memory.
Like we had this perfect love
when in reality I was dating a girl through some of it, and you were jealous,
and I didn't know what to do with it.
Then you got married on me and Rose dumped me.

I have one photo of you at the front counter at Clover Pool.

*

Your 6-1 spidery 130 pound frame sat on the sand cliffs overlooking Lake Ontario.
I sat in front of you.
Your long arms held me.

                              We didn't talk for hours.

                    *

I was 17, you were 15 when we met in the pump shop of Clover Pool.
After we'd bombed around a few weeks in my '69 Monte Carlo
                              (gold with black vinyl top)
your brother John came up to me at work: "I just want you to know Alex is gay."
I looked into his dark eyes and went back to stocking shelves.

I watch you at Don's
with the stainless steel counters and walls
eating a burger in 3 bites, your long fingers.

                    *

Walking to my car in Pasadena tonight, Christmas 2005,
not cold like Rochester.
We pissed on the door of a closed Chinese restaurant, drove on the shoulders
and the wrong sides of roads, you washed my hands in your pump shop,
saw David Bowie in the Carrier Dome, threw our empty Coke bottles
                                                    in the backseat.
By the end of summer the car chimed as we turned corners.

I asked a guy last week
if he goes to the cliffs above Hamlin Beach.
He said you can't, they're fenced off.
Can you believe it Alex? The fence and signs keep him out?

If we could meet at a summer job now when we are 17 and 15—

Walking the 11 p.m. streets of Pasadena
I thought that everything I've written has been a lie, sometimes clever
                                                    ones,
that I want to stop lying.

on hamlin beach
homage to frank o'hara and influenced by
french poets i havent read yet

alex ate a cheeseburger in four bites
long fingers white and clean—

showed their girlfriends their dicks wanted only pussy
by attacking us (flat stomachs, defined pecs, tanned!)

i released your bare foot
you moved toward them

—no, let's go.

drove my '69 monte carlo
to the next parking lot.

you massaged my neck.
o'hara's addictions
never hurt him
mine have made me
nearly straight
so i'm in rehab
of my mind
in north hollywood
with clouds.

2 kids from el salvador threaten me
cuz they like me like 2 puerto ricans
threatened o'hara because they were attracted to him.

rent is better than mortgage
because the clouds have stopped.
i have met four best minds.

with the earth
not moving
i spent the earthquake money
on javier.

the representative of the church
my parents forced me to attend
banned My Sweet Lord from the guitar mass
once a chick told him the radio version
included the Hare Krishna Mantra—
i was 10
then i Knew.

rent is better than mortgage
clouds have stopped moving against santa susana mountains
paul asks
will animals be in your afterlife?

when i die
i ask all vehicles
in los angeles
to stop for a time—
even the president's motorcade
(to see that there's not always danger).
hate to use the energy
to burn me
please put me on a pike
in the angeles national forest
for the animals and microbes.
my executor
may sell the rights
to a filmmaker to document
these stages of nature.
follow my goddamn Wishes!

and take my europe money
and give it to a whore!

Bernie's Oriole

Are there orioles
in Manhattan
without orange?
Orioles
in Manhattan
early February?

We have Frank O'Hara lunch:
"eggs mushrooms cheese whitewine grapes"

I watched 19 Nepalese hostages
executed
slow beheading of
19-year-old boy
murderers laughed
and played catch
with his head
closed eyes
twitching.

How did you get to be an adult
rejecting kids' music?
Can't help
but smile
so many
jealous of my life!

O'Hara's parents
said he looked malnourished
as he waited for them
eating 4 apples.
Getty Svaygor
broke district rules
picking me up walking to school
6th grade

Michigan winter
red VW bug—
Danny Wang
's not watching the Super Bowl either!,
Paul Murphy
's long hair
with so much white now!,
if you don't know
Keith Richards
channels Supreme Being
you still have time!
Bernie
a male English tree sparrow
hops off the tile sidewalk of Sanamluang
onto asphalt parking lot,
Mrs. Thompson
complimented my Cub Scout eyelashes
and I didn't mind,
Clapton spoke only twice at the Bowl,
"Thank you."
"Thank you."

I hate work
as much as Joe LeSueur and Frank O'Hara
I think
I can keep doing it
so we're not homeless.

KJ

white socks
bikini briefs

24-year-old virgin

cock small slender

5 inches
bent down

so many people we could love
we can't remember

you're on the bottom as we kiss
swallow the double load

know you're in love

KJ's Feet

Not a callous.
Each nail clear.
Cuticles naturally, symetrically edged.
Scent gets me hard.
Size 12.
Twenty-four.

Every other surface
(dark black hair)
perfect. Perfect scent.

You drink steadily
Absolut Cape Cod.

That monstrosity what's it called, she said.
The Pompadour Center?
Yeah that's it!
Great Rivers cardboard sculpture.

KJ your 6-foot
140 pound twink body
Nothing better in my life.
Only things equal.
The Nobel Prize in Literature
for lifetime achievement
could only equal your body
and sweet nature.
Sitting on the edge of my bed
your feet in white socks and black and white
                              tennis shoes
telling me about your boys, girls,
      computer animation free-lance.

*

[Take a good long pause here.
Take a half-hour walk or run
            or swim—break—
            then get back to this poem.
            Seriously if you don't do one
            you'll miss the experience.]

                                        *

Every night I don't look for you
but about five nights a week.
Looked through Zurich and Pattaya.

Everything disappears!

Not a hair on your chest
or flat stomach.

Rich You

I'm sorry
my material needs are met.
I have so many varied investments
that even if the world's economies collapsed
I would be rich.
Some people
can lose their fortunes
but literally I can't.

When I travel
I go alone to a new country
& hire the hottest bilingual
18-year-old boy
to show me around.

advice

how did i
get so rich.

paul spend more time in
your green grand torino.

norman send me 200 dollars a month
for the rest of your life
to try and balance
your anti-gay karma.

joe remind me your last name
come eat another load.

ron embrace lower-case
cuz i said so.

cheryl
lose.

candido
stop mumbling
jesus christ.

strange man
when you bag her
lick her pussy good.

tree
keep your peaceful consciousness
toward me.

soft-shell turtle
don't dive off the warm sand
beside the clinton river
in the drayton plains nature center
when you see me.

sarah
be a boss.

stacey
69 with me
when it's humid
in guanacaste province.

9-year-old boy
in the back seat of your family's car
on the ventura freeway
you can do it bro,
escape,
find love and happiness.

helen
go back in time
skip the farm
go to high school.

wendy
don't take acid
and get in the car
33 years ago.

enrique
don't tell me about
any of your material possessions
for 5 years.

unidentified bird
look yourself up
in peterson's fieldguide
get back to me.

diane
don't release your next book
until i edit and approve it.

rest of you
want advice
cotter1960@charter.net
you'll have to service me a while
so i can get to know you.

raul
find me again
won't let you down
this time.

it's so unfair
i'm this rich.

it's just about up

my life.
you
reading this
smiling
cuz you're alive
and i'm dead.

you don't know
in your heart
if the world will leave you
when you die.
as cheryl vossekuil says:
BUMMER!

*

i never suffered.
my nature
and my birth
michigan woods and swamps
blessed me
with peace.

For Davin

Rock band
in the alley

getting better each month.
Gonna follow the sound some night

like I did to the garage band at the end of Baybrook Drive
in Drayton Plains Michigan 1969.

Several sets of parents were scandalized
by their insistance that so many heard—

I stood before their amped instruments
beside my Stingray (leopard banana seat, sissy-bar)

knowing they were right
and the bass player, 16, very cute (I was 8).

Most of those disgruntled parents
were OK with the sounds napalm made in grass hut villages.

Five

Hi Ron Padgett!!
Never shows any poem drafts to anyone!

It's so kind of you
to respond to my emails even with two words.

I mean really
you don't need it.

Six

So Paul
we're not where we wanted to be
now that you're 46 and I'm 45
when we plotted our lives together

when you were 20 and I was 19
at Michigan State.

Yes we discussed this in your living room two weeks ago
while Anne put the kids to bed.

We might have 40 more years!
I wish I'd blown Alex

when he pulled his powder blue Rambler into the woods
when I was 19 and he was 17.

We just fogged up the windows with our breath
not talking

I'd look at his long skinny legs in worn powder blue jeans
and his crotch.

I reminded him when he was 24 and he said,
O yeah, I forgot about that.

He sat near the edge of the sand cliffs at Hamlin Beach,
I sat in front of him

and he held me with his long arms and legs
August nights

Seven

Ride your Stingray to the garage band.

Talking to the Sun

for Frank O'Hara

Coda

I'm not taking too much out Frank
to destroy this place and time.

Baby octopi float by
under glass

in bar-b-que sauce.
I have all the currency in my wallet I need Carrie!

I bought 17 shares of Johnson & Johnson online last week
for my retirement!

In 5 years of saving
I have enough to live on for 4 months

and it's perfect!

photograph of frank o'hara

cocksucker lips

Beach Taxi approaching

i'd stopped the day—

shower of coins
stepping out of cab—

parrots scream
age
from california live oaks.

straight world of commerce

fight over pizza,

cocksucking alleys

Personal Poem

for Frank O'Hara

Plane money into Javier
again.
Street hooker.
Tells me what streets I can get other boys like him
nonterritorial contractor.
WITH A LITTLE LUCK
we voted McCartney senior song
give this fifty bucks to Michael
for telling the woman she'd die
stung by a scorpion on Sugar Beach.
Javier's tiny uncut cock flopping soft as I fuck him.
John encouraged Frank to keep SECOND AVENUE going
Frank told John he'd keep SECOND AVENUE going.
\This is 27TH AVENUE.
I'm building something that can't be destroyed
Isabelle Barkell
showed me yellow violets
Michigan.
We no longer speak
Asking me to attend to wildflowers
was not to start a dialogue.
I pretend John Ashbery
wants me to keep it going.

A TRUE ACCOUNT OF TALKING TO MARLON BRANDO

when i met marlon brando
i was only a bit star struck
and immediately began asking questions.
do u read much poetry?
yes, but the minute i start reading it i get bored.

we went to a large outdoor area
of private land
i started digging with a shovel on a grassy hill
the dirt fell away easily

i continued to dig
the dirt flowing away below me
finding nothing

marlon went downhill
toward the river
and began looking around
we knew it was not our land

i wasn't sure what he was doing
he yelled at me
what kind of tree is that
i looked upriver where he was looking
there were several large trees
that i had appreciated
one clearly a 300 year old white oak
with only a few autumn leaves left
i said
the thick squat one with the large green leaves
on the upper right corner?
marlon brando shook his head yes.
i don't know i said, i think a type of eucalyptus or poplar
i have a tree book at home

we can get a leaf, look it up later.
he was satisfied with this answer and agreed and
bent back down looking at natural material by the river.

finding nothing
i gave up and moved to the top of the hill
where i found a white wall
and began digging into it.
wet drywall began to break away easily
then a wood door
which i opened
finding a small bedroom.
stapled to walls and a small corkboard
were letters and the scribblings of a teenage boy
along with a few clippings and photographs.
i began taking them down
anxious to preserve them.
it seemed to have been the abandoned room
of a boy 80 years ago.
i found a stack of old letters
one i thought from my sister lynn to him
but the light was bad
and when i reread the return address
it was only from lynn not the right last name.
then i found a compact disc
cut into a crescent moon.
so i knew the faded and yellowed material
could not be 80 years old.
and wondered if the small cabin was still being used.
i worried the owners might return
and find me trespassing
i wondered if i should take anything
so didn't take all i was interested in
just a selection of the writing, cut-outs and photographs
and i returned to brando by the river.
he had no concern about my robbery saying that u could not be an artist
if all u cared for was convention and laws.

i took down cut-outs and photographs from my grandfather's workshop
after his death.
my uncles hated him
were hiring people to tear it all down and throw it in a dumpster.
told me i could take whatever i wanted
but be fast about it.
i took small leather books where he recorded reload data, weights of bullets,
amounts of powder, velocity formulas.

marlon was 50 pounds lighter than his heaviest.
was still a very overweight man.
i was at my thinnest.
i returned to him, balding, hair mostly grey,
where he was searching with his hands
beside the mucky riverbank.

Listening to the Sun at Sanamluang Cafe

Orange Metro local
east on Sherman Way

diesel message clear

fags can marry

and those who interpret Holy Scripture otherwise are lost, lost.

That small teen you were
skinny, nearly hairless
after 2 years of football.
Be glad you crossed his path
like so many others, John Urban, John Barnes, et cetera.

Total always
Chinese porcelain rice bowls.

Because you're a citizen who supports your country's wars
eat sashimi
work for peace
and to relieve suffering.

Here's one of your wishes.

Hi Ron Padgett!!

I just wrote 2 great poems
in a Jury Room
of LA Criminal Court

with a view of the trees
and the surface of San Gabriel Mountains

they are attached
like your 2 identical twin wrestlers
from Michigan State.

I want a flock of red hotdogs in buns
to fly by out the window
dipping and gliding together

like parrots (not like pigeons and starlings)

their song
in pairs Lennon and McCartney harmonies.
Haven't seen any new dim sum in twenty years

but it keeps getting made every day.

Hi Ron Padgett!

Ron Padgett
sent me an email this morning.

Yesterday in the garage
I sorted 8 months of correspondence

saw several letters from Bob Creeley
now gone, one was about Ron Padgett!

Ron and I are surprisingly not gone
right now.

But it's coming and for most readers of this
we're already gone.

You wish you could have met us
especially Ron Padgett!

Like I wish I could have met FOH
(Ron did!!

Diane thinks she was at a party with him too
and Jerry Rothenberg was disdainful that I asked him

and said he was very small
(Jerry is 5-4!!).

(Frank was 5-7!!

Hi Ron Padgett Second Generation New York Poet

wherever you are
(New York probably!
Zurich is cold and grey

even the English tree sparrows
wish they were in LA
like the day Frank O'Hara was in Paris

thinking of Poulenc
and every person in the city was lonely
and it wasn't a projection of his inner emotional life

or a literary device
it really happened
why hasn't peace happened?

This poem may suck
but it's better than most of what the world offers.
It's peaceful and has a lot of beauty and love

though some of you will quibble with me
that prostitution doesn't inherently involve violence.
I can't write that you're a pinhead if you think that.

ballet

found
kenneth ruzicka's
home address
online
white pages—
wonder if that roman coin
flipped from his pocket
when i was 5?

want to write john ashbery
if he could give me
one of frank's possessions—
but who am i to ask

After Lunch

for Frank O'Hara

You wrote at lunch
to stay thin
so your ass looked good in pants
so everyone loved you.

I eat lunch, no one wants me,
write after. Though so many days
with your perfect ass
no one wanted you either.

Not for Poulenc but for you
I walked from Saint Germain to le Pont Mirabeau.

I was alone on that bridge
the Seine was grey
one of my exs walked with his wife
to the Avenue Mozart.

I've outlived you by 5 years
but not out-written you.
I stroll the Rue Pergolese
looking for dinner.

Good Friday

You said call you back later
I want to be alone

going to the cathedral with a friend.

Here's something new:
no symbol, no image,

presence unkind and dull.
Transcend your own life.

Mano calls

you'd love this party
(from his cell phone at the party

it's a Lebowski reunion, Goodman and Daniels
are here.

As it is I get Candido Ventura the Second.

Drug I need submissive twink.

*

Pencils are safe

mahogany phone stand
window over train tracks

Little Falls, New York.
6 tracks and the trains would shake the row house.

7, counting cars
never thought of counting boys in Los Angeles.

Loved the smell of those pencils.
Loved running to watch the trains.

Like Ashbery and O'Hara would encourage each other
to keep their long poems going—
Jerry do you think we never talked as boys

because you were being molested by Gordy
and I was a fag?

That would make sense in assembly-line
Michigan.

Angeles National Forest.
No one hears the shot

and time for animals
to consume my remains.

Let nature work in the sun.

*

I pretend John Ashbery
is encouraging me to write.

I pretend Frank O'Hara is fascinated
with what I'm writing.

The Vicodin's not bad.
Plus I have 3 Triavils for real emergencies

purple hope.

Just dropped one on the carpeted floor
can't roll far—
and I can't find it—

so hope down 33%.

Still, a hundred rounds of ammo.

*

That was John on the phone.
He loves it so far, suggests I don't stop.

When you get rid of symbol, image
and an interesting presence,

like beautiful and personal gifts you buy
before going to the beach for the weekend,

then you really gotta consider
what you're left with.

I read a few lines to Frank.
He rips me a knew one, and I still don't know

if he's a top or bottom.
All those fucking homages and memoirs

and no one gets to that gay fact.
Maybe he wasn't into anal

but no one's discussing it.
Are they being discreet?

They talk about all the hard truths he spoke
and how they loved him for it.

Diane calls, says, keep going
but it won't matter to a soul,

Bob calls
says time to cut.

Frank says Bob
cuts so much the essence is lost.

Anyone in my situation

bitches about sorrow
would have no world view.

Hank reminds me
my neighborhoods have never been bombed.

They been shot up a bit.
But no big hits.

After Ringo, Paul and I die,

I'd really love to see my first live Beatles concert.
They'd be doing some stuff

totally new.
Those boys could groove.

You gotta admit they did the art game.
You should admit it.

I keep looking in

Los Angeles, Citywide 2
my little freak Candido still there.

Had his giant dick in me 2 nights ago.

There might be reason for this.

You think drugs can't help with art

help you survive
you're a dumb-ass.

Not a plan for tomorrow.
Wonder how long I could hold out in here

doing nothing 'cept what I want?

You need me to have spiritual understanding
you're piss outta luck.

That would be another poet.
I give you flaming Kleenex.

*

I'm tired
but Frank and John want me to write on.

One of my friends
a fashion designer

takes his camera to stores
to work on knock-offs.

It's how we learn—
knocking each other off.

Forward

When he's gone
the microwave door will be closed when I get home
no blinking digital display.

Photo of
the Clinton River in Drayton Plains, Michigan
20 years before I was born.
In autumn.
Skated down it 35 years later.

Do it and let someone else find a name for it, let someone else find a name
for it, let someone else recognize it, let someone else do the dirty work.

The nurse
put oranges in a box
wrote on paper above it:
"Oranges for you,
Happy Holidays."
Roman groomed his fingers
of their juices
with his lips and tongue.

For Carrie Preston, During Lunch

I bought a blue plastic toy airplane for your landing strip.

Man who was said Shu Mai to says,
"...and 15 million goes to me.
Bonus is pretty good, 15 percent..."

I want most of the language spoken on the street   [Williams]
to shut up.

"You make me feel like a prostitute,"
Victor says.
            I think this is a good feeling for him.
At least there's poetry in Ocean Seafood
(pocket FOH, backpack Koch)

(Hi Ron Padgett!!)
and only one wants it the rest
commerce and pleasing.

Forgot my flip-flops,
put out my hand, no ashtray.   [O'Hara]

Oedipus Rex

no
night taxis
on zuma
39 years later.
wouldn't help me
to get hit by one
in the liver either.

no kenneth koch
to bring 2 empty suitcases
to my condo
no priceless manuscripts, no
a true account of talking to the sun at fire island.

you were right frank
what if nothing comes of it.
now that it has for you
what of you?
gay teens
run into the cold april surf
at zuma the 16th of 2005.

Sausage Rolls

for Manopan Prajimnork

The Last Time

I saw the primary color
toy planes
I want to land on Carrie's landing-strip
1969 at a corner store
on Watkins Lake Road in Drayton Plains, Michigan
I asked my mother about it last month
she said you could get tomato sausage there

they were behind glass
I had no money
and a strange man bought me one.

In Chinatown today
I visited 3 stores looking for small plastic planes
to send you one with the poem I wrote at lunch
(not at an Olivetti typewriter store).

Fuselage nose to tail 2 inches
wing span 2 inches—
        I think the first one that should land on you
should be green.
I never had a favorite color
but used to answer that when dumb-ass adults
(mostly teachers)
would ask.
                I think of you crying naked in your bed
in Oceanside
my hand flying the plane over your territory.

When she turned off

the soundtrack of her life
no chocolate, herb tea.

At the center of the vortex Ezra smokes.

Homeruns in the '71 All-Star Game:
Bench, Aaron, Frank Robinson, Jackson, Killebrew, Clemente.

      There's no way to clean my head
of this poison
outside
      the sub-continent of India.
      Where the food was too hot
      Ringo said.

I took *Time* magazine

to 6th grade
showing the U.S. map
with Soviet missile targets
by positions 1 through 3.
Priority 1 sites were the most important
and got the most ICBMs targeted at them.
We were glad Detroit was a 1—
we were proud of our Tigers.
But we thought the Soviets
didn't understand how important we were
outside of Pontiac, only getting a 2.
We deserved much more than the 20 ICBMs
                    pointed at us.

Day One for Jerry Kitchen

September '68
walking to 3rd grade
you from Lakewood entrance
me from Denby
as the Tigers head to the Series.

By October black-and-white TVs in every class.

Appreciating Michigan wildflowers was gay
in assembly-line Drayton Plains.

Now North Hollywood
and somewhere in Michigan around a GM plant.
29 more years have passed
We hold on
              purest chance
                      trilliums left
where Cooley meets the Nature Center
moving shoots toward snow.
By you today a hepatica in bloom.
We won't see it because we have plans.

Did I ever show you
the hepatica I transplanted to my tree garden?
Did I ever show you
Isabelle Barkell's transplanted yellow violet?

I pick a lavendar hepatica blossom
stem thinner than a toothpick
lay it on the straight European porn magazine
you'd hid in the basement of the abandoned house.

hitting snooze

this morning
before fully awake
i made a dream
the snooze button
might give a great reward

so in semi-sleep i
hit it five times
instead of the usual 2
thinking i might win
a great prize

but was only
late for work.

mom—

the boy
doesn't want
another spoonful of steamed
buddha brand jasmine rice—
he reaches for a chopstick
propped on a bowl of tom yum instead.
    now
tapping the stick everywhere
and waving it in the air
he accepts a spoonful of red fish.

New Year's Day 2005

I don't have time for 200 year old oaks.

No one loves me today
the way I want to be loved—
still
perfect.
I failed so much
last year—today
still perfect.

Cumulonimbus and
diffusing contrails.
Most of you
have so little peace.
I'm sending you some
today—I mysteriously
have so much to share today.

New Year's Resolution 2005

Next year I resolve
to increase my use of boy whores,
gain 50 pounds,
and create significant credit card debt.

nothing

the waffle iron
of the queen mary
makes unsymmetric wedges.

fanatics know
how many pounds of spaghetti
in the bucket
john lennon forks to the fat woman
in Magical Mystery Tour
but they can't prove it.

[one minute pause]

online profile check-boxes
and room for narrative
to help you choose me.

that a big noodle?
she asks.
fair question.

[one minute pause]

"You wanna try some
it's got a very nice flavor
but a little bit on the greasy side?"

[one minute pause]

the teenage boy fingers
his father's change, bills and coins.
abstractions
        pain teenagers to their growing bones.

dad let's him calculate a tip
pocket the rest

he blows a straw wrapper
at his father's face
then places it on his arm,
then strokes his ear and cheek with it.

pizzeria sol y luna

last sunlight
table on broken street
view of flamingo bay

kids barefoot
carrying apricot sized tops
pulled w/ string

white pick-up
16
sitting in bed
barefoot
yellow baseball cap in reverse
yellow t
smoking filtered cigarette.

sun about done

more children come out to play.
day has cooled.

—Brasilito, Costa Rica

rice balls for son

some
facial hair
of undergrad boys
is wrong.

clouds never so.
a whole bay
in costa rica
to myself last summer.

how did
i get myself there
feeding mosquitos?

with no LA light pollution
stars
black ocean
heat broke.

marlom tired
after 16 hours
serving pork
rice, beans, guanabana.

mother makes a rice ball
3 centimeters in diameter
places it in the mouth
of her 2-year-old son.

he watches her palms
roll the next rice ball.

Shit shit shit!

I left the safe open
with a .44 magnum, over a hundred rounds of ammo,
two .308s, couple hundred rounds of ammo,
thousand dollars of earthquake cash
all in twenties,
the gold eagle Mano got me for helping him with his green card,
the coins my grandmother gave me,
Mano's jewelry, Arthea's credit cards,
coins I bought
including one of the best 1909 VDB-S
Lincoln pennies in existence.

shadow

live-oak
california scrub
waxy sharp almond size leaves
couple brown 16 year old boys
in thailand mating.
hybrids
        interest
skeleton fingers move
with vessels and tendons
package—   the live-oak
the bill the getting by on money
.

       sensing consciousness
t-waves killdeer stick legs
grass.
     dissolve
all concrete structures
during earthquake. running
seal barks, looters of imagination
.

       touching worst memories
they're best left buried this
is not helpful. the basket already hit
deflating balloon floating to ground.
sound all syllables eternity,
walk to the sea
for free salt. walk to selma.
trenches, artillery drawn, general-
s exchange black-eyed Susan.
     delicate
consistent controlled explosions.
shore you don't hear or see
worms and crabs. hammer dents
primer creates no spark—or a
somehow slow burn hold the barrel.

excitement of the ones that don't go off
pliers removing bullet from case.
removing the live shell from the chamber
calcium exoskeletons
wet lips unpowdered, runny nose scholar
licking the crack
of an old professor.
so many children's toys spin
i get dizzy.

       9 billion years of stasis
and nowhere to go.
         rocks we make revolving
times the speed of sound.
         military fighters.
         we used to drop leaflets before our fire storms
before our blockbusters and atom bombs,
before vaporizing our enemies
or scattering them cellularly—but now most of our enemies are illiterate
so we just bring them the goods
as they're studying a live-oak
looking the sky over,
passing a flower, whipping the kid, butchering animals,
planting a seed, moving a door, smashing mites.
good morning from my country.

Sausage roll

wrapped in wax paper
in my sweatshirt pocket
Paris—
    Mano
can't bring you sausage rolls
they'd lose so much in the day back to LA.
   This un-
flashy neighborhood
by the National Archive,
Boulangerie Patisserie

Two university students cruise me
one my type—
                  so the game's not over yet.
Boy's cell
jammed into motorcycle helmet—
This poem
might get me a university job!
I have 3 Franks
for emergency purposes only
                      folded in my pocket
(Joe's Jacket, For Grace, After a Party, Why I Am Not a Painter)
—there will likely be emergencies soon—

                *

           In New York loft
trying to unbotton Alex's jeans—
(was to suck his cock).
           A decade later
he asked me to join him
with his wife in bed.
         OK
but wish you had come to LA—
Man-purse walks by again—27—
5 day beard—

Did Guillaume think his loves flowed down the Siene
and never came back?
When I stood on le Pont Mirabeau yesterday
I saw green water
not my past loves
    (Alex, Leah, Mark, John, Joe, John, Rose
    Ginger, Paula, Sarah, Rico, Aaron, Greta,
    Daryl, KJ, Manopan...)
I think Greta just came back
in steam
          through coffee grounds
                    of café crème.
              *

On Rue des Archives
I want to be lovers with 20 men that walk by
and 2 women.
(They thought Monet always loved!)

I'll carry a baguette
in a wax bag
walking to the Metro
out of Paris
(as a man in an orange coat sings.

Direct Poems

for Bernie White

for bob creeley 5/1/05

i said to him
you prolly want me to speed it along

"...as you say I'd say, see if you can quicken it
somehow, keep it moving. Onward!

Best as ever,
Bob"

Fake Smile

Don't fake smile
Don't get fat like me
Don't use periods in this poem
But pause at the end of every line anyway
Don't rip people a new one Diane

Work for the material world
your suffering increases
    Be de-linked from possessions
in your nice house
give things to the poor. Don't
define yourself by negation. Listen
(like the button said) to The Beatles
Do you keep falling in love with people that don't want you
or are dead? are your favorite family members dead?
Ron the caps and so much else are fucked in this poem.
Definitely be alone instead of with people
        who fake smile
        and talk
        to fill space
        Can you dig it?
Most tiles are undesirable.
He's mostly a hero who loves you.
Don't you want to know if Rico is available—
Use dashes as dashes and instead of question marks.
Even if you get stood-up on a pole
        with your grave behind you
        and shot

There are still answers.
Soon as you know you're mortal you know you're dead.
Three of my grandparents
watched all of their siblings and friends die
Save 2 tablespoons of Pad Thai.
Don't kill, steal and rape.

Don't physically attack people (self-defense is different).
Pre-emptive war, why not, if you're right.
Don't wait for some of you to get murdered to act.
Don't run away if you're a pacifist.

direct poem

for bernie white

it's all i could've done.
    our discomfort
not comparable
to those truly suffering.
    this is incorrect
and lacking—
    but it's for you
is the access free enough?
we'll disappear
like a man who died
at age 17
in what is now nebraska
in 1327
we'll never know anything about him.
we're in peace and
free from suffering.
i jacked off 6 times yesterday
between 4 p.m. and midnight
each time dreaming of a man
i don't have
remembering a real guy, making
composites of guys,
creating imaginary guys.
here's your art.
is it satisfying
with no puffy clouds?

MSU, 1978

his porsche
navy
rag top

dogwood fluff
blows across it

freezes you
richest & beauty

MSU, 1979

his porsche
navy
rag top

dogwood fluff
blows across

freezes you
riches & beauty

Green

Did you ever
get the list of whores
in your green book
all simultaneously mad at you?

They all call each other
on the whore partyline.

Boy then you know you're spiraling.

editors' comments on rejection from café review:

NO BS odd—
No to ALL
   but at least
   interesting MM
NO—KB

Apology

I'm sorry
my material needs are met.
I have so many varied investments
even if the world's economies collapse
I'm rich.
Some people
can lose their fortunes
but literally I can't.

I hire the hottest 18-year-old
as a guide
when I travel alone
to a new country.

When youth is gone

When youth is gone
and you figured no way to acquire
          power and money
stand beside a road
selling 2 bunches of wild scallions tied
               with discarded twine
on the border of Thailand and Burma.

you're painting me

you're painting me
stop painting me
i'm not a wall
(dad wiping
4-year-old son's face
with a paper napkin).

zuma

hair in armpits of 13,
none in 9,
but 9's feet
same size
.
both carry
leafless strands
tubular green
to hole they're digging
.
kelp ropes
piled pollock style
asses and feet
in the air as they dig

Afterword

Finding Frank

by Craig Cotter

Frank O'Hara's mock-manifesto "Personism" taught me that a poem doesn't have to have a big-bang at the end where I'm going to change your life with my brilliance. A poem can simply be a message to a friend full of personal references. People can figure-it-out or not.

This idea gave my writing new freedom—blast away and ignore the old rules of the self-contained machine.

O'Hara's poem "At the Old Place" begins:

> Joe is restless and so am I, so restless,
> Button's buddy lips frame "L G T TH O P?"
> across the bar. "Yes!" I cry, for dancing's
> my soul delight. (Feet! feet!) "Come on!"

In Joe LeSueur's *Some Digressions on Poems by Frank O'Hara: A Memoir*, he tells us that "L G T TH O P" stood for "Let's go to the Old Place," another gay club. After reading the LeSueur key, I kept rereading the poem thinking—I suppose an excellent reader of poetry could've figured-out that "L G T TH O P" was a lipped communication across a loud bar to get out of here—but I also thought I would have never gotten it. I'm grateful LeSueur showed me a way in.

For my poetry to move forward using O'Hara's lessons, I've included notes to save readers from having to search for references that might be difficult to find. (Is anything difficult to find anymore with the Internet?)

*

Before stumbling onto LeSueur's book—decades before—I'd been briefly exposed to O'Hara's poetry studying English at Michigan State University in 1979. I was told about the romantic poet who had been silly enough to fall asleep on a beach at night and had his head run over by a dune buggy. (Frank's actual death was nothing like that.)

I remember looking at *Lunch Poems* and not getting it.

No one mentioned to me that Frank was gay.

With LeSueur's brilliant book, O'Hara's poetry became accessible for the first time. I became insatiable for information about Frank's life. I read every book of theory, his other writings, memoirs. And I wanted to meet his friends.

I found Vincent Warren—Frank's last boyfriend—who left New York shortly before Frank's death in 1966 to become the principal dancer of Les Grands Ballets Canadiens de Montreal for 15 years. When I sent him an email he had retired from dancing and had become the Ballet's archivist. He sent me a wonderful email of remembrances.

I searched for Bill Berkson. After a few nervous months of trying to craft a letter that didn't sound insane, I finally put one in the mail asking if we could meet in San Francisco. Bill kindly agreed.

I left LA at 6 a.m. and drove to the French restaurant Bill selected—we met at 2 p.m. My case of nerves continued: "This is kind of odd," I said, "when you meet someone new you usually start with pleasantries, but we only have two hours." I had 9 pages of written questions. In a kind and friendly voice, smiling, he said, "Go ahead with your questions."

Meeting Bill Berkson on a perfect summer day in San Francisco in 2012 was one of the great highlights of my life. Frank was known for holding nothing back—speaking his mind at all times—sometimes cruelly. But his friends who shared so many memories of their time with him were rarely so direct in their published accounts. I had many questions about Frank's homosexuality, private relationships, and how these parts of his biography may have shaped his art. Bill spoke in such an open, honest, and direct way, I immediately knew why he was a friend of Frank's. I could understand why

96

Frank cared so much about Bill. "It was so long ago," Bill said at one point. "You know, for years I could impersonate Frank, the distinctive way he talked." Bill gave me an immediate sense of their take-no-prisoners, serious discussions of art, tempered, as so many of O'Hara's poems are, with a wicked, campy sense of humor.

I think what moves me most about Frank's biography is that he lived "out" and was unapologetic about being homosexual before Stonewall—before "gay—" before the Gay Rights Movement. He was often flamboyant— what we might now call "fem." That was particularly brave because such "out" behavior in the 1950s and '60s brought with it real safety risks, from getting beat-up to losing apartments and jobs. As I was learning about O'Hara's insistence to live on his own terms, it sent me reeling back to my first inklings of being gay at age 11—in a Michigan neighborhood in the early '70s that had no out gay people—where cock-suckers needed to be beat-up or sent to asylums for shock treatments. If only those living open gay lives in New York had told us in Drayton Plains, Michigan about it. Frank had—in his brilliant poems—but they had not made it to me in suburban Detroit.

My *After Lunch* title is certainly a play on, and reference to, O'Hara's *Lunch Poems*. How does one continue after *Lunch*? After O'Hara? How do we move forward with our poetry respecting what he taught us—wear those tight pants that make our asses look good so everyone will love us—how to be out, unapologetic, and get it in the art?

I've attempted a few triple riffs. O'Hara's "True Account" poem riffs off of Mayakovsky's "An Extraordinary Adventure Which Happened To Me, Vladimir Mayakovsky, One Summer In The Country." This type of "true account" poem is actually quite self-aggrandizing as the sun tells you you're a pretty swell poet. After several failed attempts I decided to split the difference between two poems, one talking to Marlon Brando, the other *listening* to the sun at Sanamluang Café in North Hollywood.

Another triple riff comes as I learned how O'Hara's "For Poulenc" references Apollionaire's "La Pont Mirabeau." I'm hoping that the title poem of this book carries the tradition forward.

*

"For Poulenc" documents a walk O'Hara took on his first day in Paris. As part of my O'Hara immersion I called my friend from our Michigan State days, Mark Rabinowitz, who now lives in Zurich. I showed him the poem, asked him to get out a map and draw the walk. (I also invited myself to visit Mark and have him take me to Paris—he generously agreed.)

My first entry into Paris began at St. Germain; we stopped on the Pont Mirabeau (where a man was reading a book of Apollinaire poems); and we ended in rue Pergolèse (with the tobacco and the nuns). That boy could walk—the route was nearly 9 miles—a perfect way to enter Paris for the first time. As I stood on that bridge—where Apollinaire and O'Hara stood—our past loves flowing away down the Seine—I wanted to have dinner and then go for a walk with O'Hara. That is the setting for these poems.

The chance that a time machine will be invented in my lifetime seems about zero; the chance that I'll get to meet Frank (and Lennon and Harrison) in an afterlife seems about zero; fortunately we have this time machine and afterlife called poetry.

Notes on the Poems

Dear Carrie

—"Blander" —Type of turtle native to the Great Lakes area, also known as "Blanding's Turtle" (Emys blandingii).

—"hepatica" —Wildflower in woodlands of the eastern United States. Often the first wildflower to bloom in the spring, sometimes blooming through melting snow.

—"Pra Pathom Chedi" —Buddhist temple an hour from Bangkok, thought to house the oldest Buddhist structure in Thailand, a chedi (pagoda) over 2000 years old.

—"Doi Suthep" —Used here as the name of the temple Wat Prathat Doi Suthep. Doi Suthep is a mountain near Chiang Mai in northern Thailand. The steps of this temple (and Naka handrails) are shown in the film *Beautiful Boxer*.

—"Frank O'Hara" and "lanolin" —In Joe LeSueur's stunning memoir of Frank O'Hara, *Digressions on Some Poems by Frank O'Hara*, he remembers that his roommate (and sometimes lover) always had "...little tubes of lanolin ointment...around the house. Convinced that it did wonders for your skin..." As LeSueur indicates, lanolin shows up in several of FOH's poems, including "Sonnet," "V. R. Lang," and "Biotherm (For Bill Berkson)." LeSueur: "What was it with Frank and his thing about lanolin? I draw a blank; I wish someone would enlighten me."

—"Intermediate Period" —periods of anarchy—interruptions of Pharaonic rule—in Ancient Egypt.

—"Tolstoy gave one-and-a-half pages..." —from *War and Peace*.

Advice for Carrie Preston

—"Mano" —Manopan Prajimnork, Bangkok, Thailand; Pasadena, California, U.S.A.

—"...Allen Ginsberg refused to defend..." —In one of the last interviews before his death, Ginsberg was asked, "What does it mean, 'I saw the best minds of my generation destroyed by madness, starving/hysterical naked...'?" Ginsberg replied: "It means I saw the best minds of my generation destroyed by madness, starving/hysterical naked..."

—"The young boy Plato..." —"La Jeunesse d'Aristotle," "The Youth of Aristotle (1875)," a spectacular sculpture by Charles Degorge (1837-1888) in the Musée d'Orsay, Paris.

—"the train station" —The Musée d'Orsay was originally a train station.

—"Goo' night sweet lady" —A variation from Part II of Eliot's "Wasteland," "A Game of Chess."

For Alex

—"Monte Carlo" —Auto built by Chevrolet (General Motors), 1970-1988 and 1995 to the present. This poem references a 1969 Monte Carlo—a few actually do exist as the 1970 Monte Carlo was introduced on September 18, 1969.

—"Don's" —Don's Original, 4900 Culver Rd., Sea Breeze, Rochester, New York

—"Pasadena" —Pasadena, California

—"Carrier Dome" —At Syracuse University

—"Hamlin Beach" —Hamlin Beach State Park is on the south side of Lake Ontario 25 miles northwest of Rochester, New York. The 1223 acre park includes a half mile of sand beach.

on hamlin beach
homage to frank o'hara and influenced by french poets i haven't read yet

—"threatened o'hara because they were attracted to him." —In *City Poet*, a biography of the life and times of Frank O'Hara by Brad Gooch, the author recounts an incident of O'Hara's being heckled by a group of Puerto Rican boys and the poet's response as, "It means they think we're attractive."

—"… four best minds…" —a reference to "Howl" by Allen Ginsberg: "I saw the best minds of my generation destroyed by madness, starving hysterical naked."

Bernie's Oriole

—"eggs mushrooms cheese whitewine grapes" —From the O'Hara poem "The Lunch Hour," 1961.

Friends and I have prepared several Frank O'Hara lunches. We read his poems during a meal made with only the 5 ingredients above.

—"19 Napalese hostages" —The video of their execution in Iraq in 2005 can be found on the Internet. They had traveled to Iraq to make money as food workers. They were murdered by men who felt they were part of a U.S. occupying force.

I hope that the murderers are imprisoned for life for their senseless slaughter of innocents.

—"Sanamluang" —In this case, Sanamluang Cafe on Sherman Way in North Hollywood, California. Sister restaurant on Hollywood Boulevard in Hollywood, California. Original reference, the large field (Sanam) beside the Royal (Luang) Palace in Bangkok, Thailand.

—"Bowl" —The Hollywood Bowl.

advice

—In this poem, as an exercise, I decided to explore a taboo, and selected unsolicited advice. I gave myself the task of using a highly arrogant voice and giving unsolicited advice to my closest friends and family members. Although one friend didn't want to read my advice to her, I was surprised to find that the rest enjoyed the advice. Several friends commissioned personal advice poems.

—"grand torino" —The Ford Torino was a car produced by the Ford Motor Company for the North American market between 1968 and 1976. The Grand Torino was a member of that line from 1972-1976.

—"guanacaste province" —The rural, forested north-west province of Costa Rica bordering the Pacific Ocean.

Coda

—"...taking too much out..." —Frank O'Hara once said that Robert Creeley, in attempts to arrive at crispness of language and clarity of experience, often pared-down poems too much, thus depriving them of feeling.

—"...float by/under glass..." —Dim sum

photograph of frank o'hara

—"Beach Taxi" —Frank O'Hara died the day after being hit by a beach taxi on Fire Island, July 25, 1966.

—"shower of coins" —The last time Joe LeSeuer saw Frank O'Hara, July 20, 1966, they shared a cab home after a performance of Stravinsky's *Oedipus Rex* at Lincoln Center's Philharmonic Hall. Instead of paying half the fare for the cab, O'Hara simply got out of the cab and showered LeSeuer with all the money he had.

Listening to the Sun at Sanamluang Cafe

Riffing off the Frank O'Hara poem "A True Account of Talking to the Sun at Fire Island," which was riffing off the Mayakovsky poem "An Extraordinary Adventure Which Befell Vladimir Mayakovsky In A Summer Cottage."

I'd encourage anyone to attempt writing a "talking to the sun poem" as the form is very difficult. The sun must involve a sense of an omnipotent voice—and, even more difficult—there is a self-aggrandizing aspect to this form as "god" will essentially be telling you (poet) that you and your work are really quite good!

I so far haven't been a great enough writer to talk to the sun—so am working my way up by listening.

—"Sanamluang Cafe" —An authentic Thai restaurant at 12980 Sherman Way, North Hollywood, CA. Original reference, the large field (Sanam) beside the Royal (Luang) Palace in Bangkok, Thailand.

—"Orange Metro local" —a bus

Hi Ron Padgett Second Generation New York Poet

—"thinking of Poulenc" —See the O'Hara poem "For Poulenc," written in 1963 when he was 37.

—"Poulenc" —Francis Jean Marcel Poulenc (January 7, 1899—January 30, 1963) was a French composer and member of the French group Les Six.

—"For Poulenc" —The great poem written by Frank O'Hara in 1963 at age 37. It describes his first walk through Paris. Many friends helped me reproduce that exact walk on my first day in Paris in the fall of 2005.

ballet

—"kenneth ruzicka" —Rizucka, when a young man, hit Frank O'Hara with his off-duty beach taxi on Fire Island in 1966. This accident resulted in

O'Hara's death 24 hours later.

—"roman coin" —Frank O'Hara carried an old Roman coin and a bolt-end broken from a packing crate (used to ship Musem of Modern Art paintings to exhibits in Europe) as good luck charms. His friends wondered if he was carrying either on the day he was fatally injured. Neither charm was ever found.

After Lunch

—See Frank O'Hara's "Personism: A Manifesto." "As for measure and other technical apparatus, that's just common sense: if you're going to buy a pair of pants you want them to be tight enough so everyone will want to go to bed with you."

—See the Frank O'Hara Poem "For Poulenc." With the help of many friends, my first hours in Paris in 2005 followed the route described in this poem. I also have 10 pages of letters from friends about how to accomplish this walk in keeping with the O'Hara poem and considering Apollinaire's poem "Le Pont Mirabeau."

—"le Pont Mirabeau" —A bridge across the Seine in Paris, mentioned in Apollinaire's poem "La Pont Mirabeau" (try the Ron Padgett translation), and also referenced through Apollinaire in the O'Hara Poem "For Poulenc." (Francis Jean Marcel Poulenc [January 7, 1899—January 30, 1963] was a French composer and member of the French group Les Six.)

Good Friday

As Brad Gooch points-out in *City Poet*, it was Kenneth Koch, not John Ashbery, who encouraged O'Hara to keep his long poem "Second Avenue" going (and not his poem "Easter"). Koch was working on his own long poem "When the Sun Tries to Go On," while Ashbery was working on his long poem "Petroleum Lima Beans."

Forward

—"When he's gone..." —My roommate Manopan Prajimnork often leaves the microwave active when he leaves our apartment. This annoyed me at first. One day I realized if he weren't in my life the microwave would be off when I returned home each day. Now I acknowledge our long friendship when I see the vent door open and the lights blinking on our microwave.

—"Oranges for you..." —Story told to me by Roman Lopez-Carlos.

For Carrie Preston, During Lunch

—"Shu Mai" —Shu Mai (sometimes spelled Sui Mai) is a type of dim sum ("heart's delight"). The expression means "cook and sell," so Shu Mai can be almost anything, but generally in a dim sum restaurant is a chewy pork meatball in a thin wheat flour or gyoza wrapper.

—"...language spoken on the street..." —I have a cassette of a William Carlos Williams reading, undated, that was recorded for me by the Michigan State University Library in 1980. After reading the short poems "To Greet A Letter-Carrier" (1938) and "At the Bar (1938)," Williams says, "I think that poetry comes out of the language that is spoken on the street."

—"Ocean Seafood" —Ocean Seafood Restaurant, 750 North Hill Street, Los Angeles, CA 90012 (in Chinatown).

—"(Hi Ron Padgett!!) —Hi Ron Padgett!!!

—"...put out my hand, no ashtray." —a reference to O'Hara's poem "For Grace, After a Party," written in 1954 at age 28.

Oedipus Rex

Frank O'Hara died on July 25, 1966. When a friend, J. J. Mitchell, opened his beach bag, he found a small journal with a single entry on the first page. As author Brad Gooch describes in *City Poet*, "It was a poem in O'Hara's own handsomely vertical writing titled "Oedipus Rex—"evidently inspired by Stravinsky's opera, for which Larry Rivers was designing sets at the time. The poem was O'Hara's last.

The Last Time

—"(not at an Olivetti typewriter store)." —There was an Olivetti typewriter showroom close to where O'Hara worked at the Museum of Modern Art in New York. Often at lunch he would walk next door, and, as he described in his note to *Lunch Poems*:

> "Often this poet, strolling through the noisy splintered glare of a Manhattan noon, has paused at a sample Olivetti to type up thirty or forty lines of ruminations...to limn his computed misunderstandings of the eternal questions of life, co-existence and depth, while never forgetting to eat Lunch his favorite meal."

When she turned off

—"Ezra smokes" —See Pound's "Vorticism," *Fortnightly Review*, 1914.

—"The Who" —The British rock band destroyed many of its instruments during and at the conclusion of concerts. During the band's early years the members were always broke—and had to beg music stores for credit to buy new instruments after shows.

—"middle-lattitude" —The middle lattitudes are the areas between 30 and 60 degrees north latitude and 30 and 60 degrees south, or, roughly, the earth's temperate zones between the tropics and the Arctic and Antarctic. (Wikipedia free encyclopedia).

—"All-Star Game" —See Major League Baseball, the United States of America.

—"Ringo" —See Richard Starkey, a.k.a. Ringo Starr, drummer for the rock band The Beatles. See also the band's trip to Rishikesh, Uttar Pradesh, India to study transcendental meditation with the Maharishi Mahesh Yogi in 1968.

Day One for Jerry Kitchen

—"Tigers" —The Detroit Tigers won the 1968 World Series, beating the St. Louis Cardinals in 7 games.

—"trilliums" —Also known as the Snow Trillium (trillium grandiflorum), a herbaceous perennial that grows in woods (that have never been cleared) from Quebec to Georgia (U.S.).

—"Cooley" —Thomas M. Cooley Elementary School, 2000 Highfield Rd., Waterford, MI 48329.

—"Nature Center" —The Drayton Plains Nature Center, 2125 Denby, Waterford, MI. 137 acres of woods, fields and ponds beside the Clinton River. It is a private-non-profit trying to hold-on against developers—send them a tax-deductible buck.

—"hepatica" —Wildflower in woodlands of the eastern United States. Often the first wildflower to bloom in the spring, sometimes blooming through melting snow.

hitting snooze

This poem is dedicated to Diane Wakoski. Diane has written many lovely poems about gambling, which she considers a metaphor for democracy, in her collection *The Emerald City of Las Vegas*.

pizzeria sol y luna

—"sol y luna" —Spanish for "sun and moon."

shadow

—"live-oak" —The California Live Oak (*Quercus agrifolia*), also known as the Coast Live Oak, is an evergreen oak native to the coastal regions of southwestern North America.

—"t-waves" —Earthquakes create waves that travel through the earth. P (primary) waves are the fastest, and move through solids and liquids. S (secondary) waves travel only through solid materials. T (tertiary) waves can travel thousands of miles within a layer of the upper ocean called the SOFAR channel. T-waves occur during earthquakes under oceans. Some believe that animals—especially birds—can detect the approach of an earthquake by sensing T-waves.

—"killdeer" — *Charadrius vociferus,* the most common American plover. (It's a bird!)

—"walk to the sea/for free salt..." —During their colonial occupation, the British charged the poor in India a salt tax. Mahatma Gandhi considered this, and all of British rule, a curse. On March 12, 1930, he left Sabarmati Ashram with 78 followers and began his 241 mile walk to Dandi on the sea to make free salt. All along the way he spoke, and people joined his march. On April 5 he arrived at Dandi, prayed, addressed the crowd, and at 8:30 a.m. he picked up a small lump of natural salt. Gandhi had broken the law. Followers everywhere followed suit, and within one week the jails of India were full. Gandhi was also arrested and jailed. This act of civil disobedience received worldwide attention. After being released from prison in 1930, Lord Irwin invited Gandhi to New Delhi for talks about Indian independence.

—"walk to selma" —Three civil rights marches from Selma to Montgomery, Alabama, occurred in 1965. The first march, on March 7, led by John Lewis and Hosea Williams, made it only 6 blocks before law enforcement brutally attacked the peaceful marchers with clubs, tear gas and bull whips. Seventeen marchers were hospitalized, leading to the naming of the day "Bloody Sunday." The second march was on March 9, 1965, led by Martin Luther King. A federal district court issued a restraining order preventing the march. King led marchers to the Edmund Pettus Bridge, held a prayer session, and turned the marchers back. Soon after, the same judge who was considering the march issue, ruled in favor of the marchers. The third march, on March 21, 1965, began with 3200 marchers but grew to 25,000 by the second day. On the state capitol steps, Martin Luther King gave his "How Long, Not Long" speech. Within 5 months President Johnson had signed the Voting Rights Act of 1965.

for bob creeley 5/1/06

I didn't know that Robert Creeley was seriously ill when I received what would be his last email. The final 4 lines, with exact line breaks, are from that email.

About the Poet

Craig Cotter was born in 1960 in New York and has lived in California since 1986. He is the author of three collections of poetry, including *Chopstix Numbers*. *After Lunch with Frank OHara* was a finalist for the National Poetry Series. Poems from *After Lunch with Frank O'Hara* have appeared in *Global Tapestry Review, poems-for-all, Poetry New Zealand, Assaracus, Court Green, Eleven Eleven, Euphony, The Antigonish Review* and *Caliban Online*. Fifteen of his poems were nominated for Pushcart Prizes from 2009 to 2013. He is online at www.craigcotter.com.

CPSIA information can be obtained at www.ICGtesting.com
Printed in the USA
BVOW11s1735250614

357337BV00012B/943/P